Oliver Tarney

MISSA MEDIA NOCTE

FOR SATB (WITH DIVISIONS) AND ORGAN OR CHAMBER ENSEMBLE

VOCAL SCORE

MUSIC DEPARTMENT

OXFORD
UNIVERSITY PRESS

OXFORD
UNIVERSITY PRESS

Great Clarendon Street, Oxford OX2 6DP,
United Kingdom

Oxford University Press is a department of the University of Oxford.
It furthers the University's objective of excellence in research, scholarship,
and education by publishing worldwide. Oxford is a registered trade mark of
Oxford University Press in the UK and in certain other countries

First published 2019

Impression: 1

ISBN 978-0-19-353048-5

Music and text origination by John Duggan at Sparks Publishing Services Ltd

Printed in Great Britain on acid-free paper by
Halstan & Co. Ltd, Amersham, Bucks.

Contents

Composer's note

Missa media nocte was commissioned for the 2017 Midnight Mass at Lancaster Priory. It is a short, celebratory work, incorporating four French carols: 'Noël Nouvelet' (*Kyrie*); 'Quelle est cette odeur agréable?' (*Gloria*); 'Quittez, pasteurs' (*Sanctus and Benedictus*); and 'Il est né le divin enfant' (*Agnus Dei*). These melodies also belong to English hymns from different parts of the Church year, which means the mass can be used whenever a short festal setting is required; however, the organ accompaniment can be extended by glockenspiel, trumpet, timpani, and percussion to make it particularly suitable for the celebration of Christmas.

This note may be reproduced as required for programme notes.

Instrumentation

Trumpet in B♭
Timpani
Percussion (player 1: suspended cymbal and triangle; player 2: glockenspiel)
Organ

The organ is always required to accompany the mass, but the addition of trumpet, glockenspiel, or timpani, in any combination, will add further colour to the performance. Suspended cymbal and triangle can also be added, but not in isolation.

The instrumental parts are available for purchase (ISBN 978–0–19–353049–2).

Duration: *c.*10 minutes

for Don Gillthorpe and the choir of Lancaster Priory

Missa Media Nocte

1. Kyrie

OLIVER TARNEY

First performed by the choir of Lancaster Priory, conductor Don Gillthorpe, on 24 December 2017.

Printed in Great Britain

OXFORD UNIVERSITY PRESS, MUSIC DEPARTMENT, GREAT CLARENDON STREET, OXFORD OX2 6DP

2. Gloria

* If accompanied by organ only, start at bar 11.

3. Sanctus and Benedictus

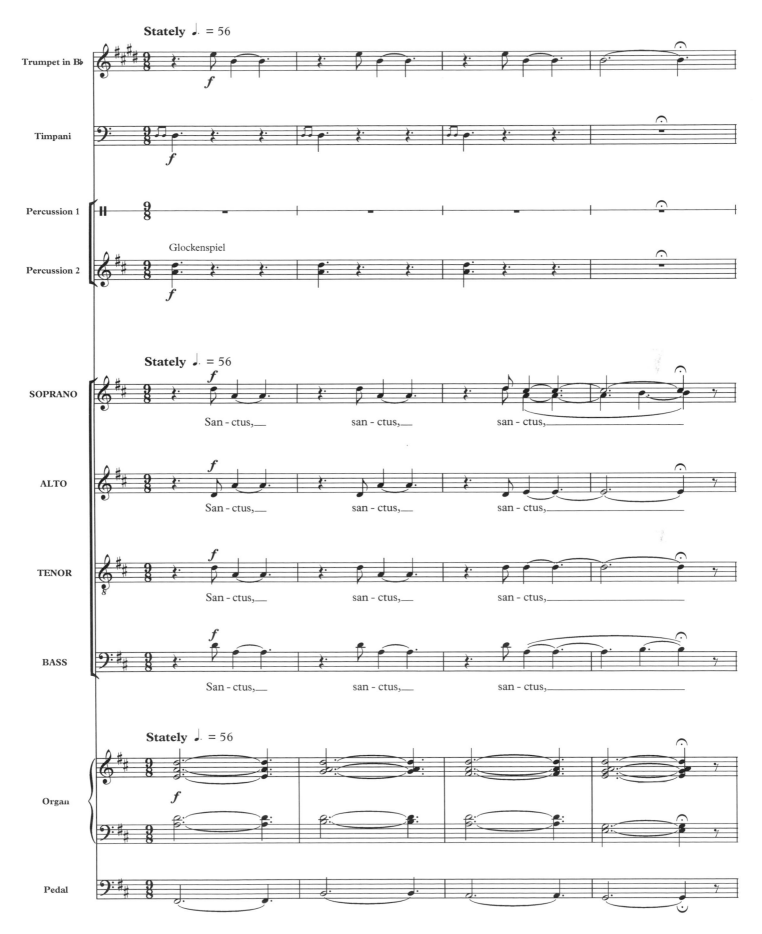

* in case of one manual

4. Agnus Dei

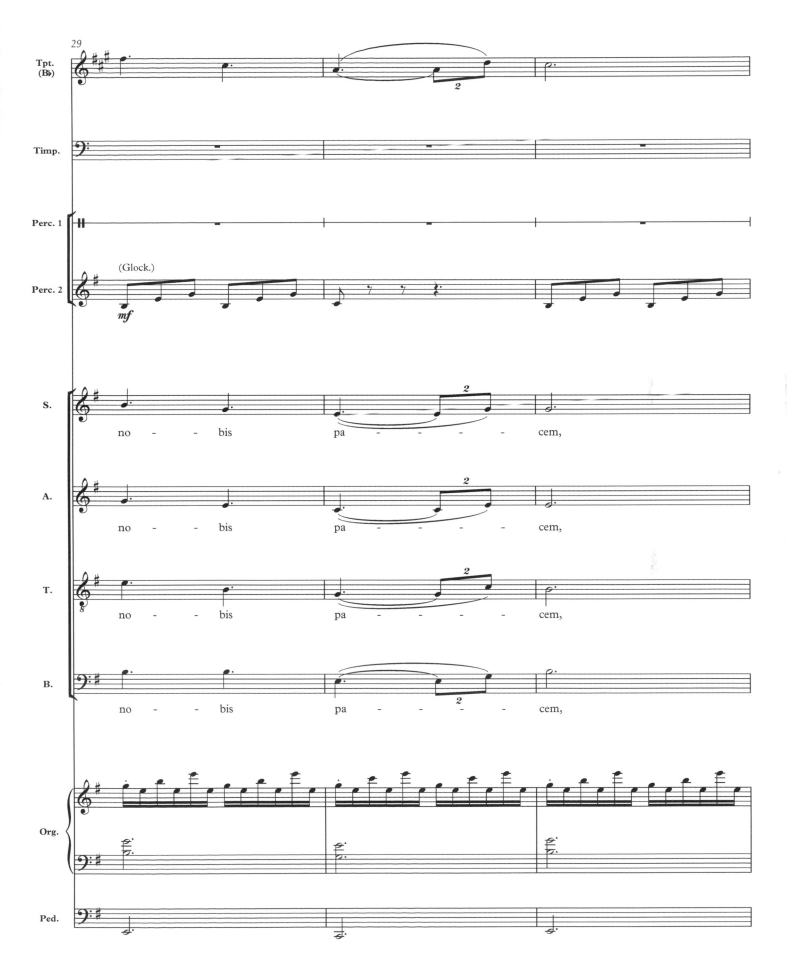